THE TEACHING-LEARNING UNIT

The Instructional Design Library

Volume 18

THE TEACHING-LEARNING UNIT

Harold F. Rahmlow
The American College
Bryn Mawr, Pennsylvania

Danny G. Langdon
Series Editor

Educational Technology Publications
Englewood Cliffs, New Jersey 07632

Westinghouse Learning Corporation PLAN* Teaching-Learning Units appearing in Appendix 2 of this volume are reprinted with the permission of Westinghouse Learning Corporation, Pittsburgh, Pennsylvania.

Library of Congress Cataloging in Publication Data

Rahmlow, Harold F
    The teaching-learning unit.

    (The Instructional design library; v. no. 18)
    Bibliography: p.49-50,
    1. Individualized instruction. I. Title. II. Series.
LB1031.R33   371.39'4   77-25107
ISBN 0-87778-122-2

Printed in the United States of America.

Library of Congress Catalog Card Number:
77-25107.

International Standard Book Number:
0-87778-122-2.

First Printing: February, 1978.

FOREWORD

The Teaching-Learning Unit (TLU) is an instructional design that grew out of a highly organized, systematic, computer based, total instructional system (Project PLAN). It is the result of thousands of hours of work with many students.

One of the aspects of this design that both teachers and students will find of benefit is the manner in which TLUs can be modified to meet particular needs. This is especially true in the way it can be modified to meet different levels of student study. Thus, a wide range of application is possible, from elementary to advanced levels of education.

Finally, I think it is important to stress the importance which is given in TLUs to simplicity of design, which is necessary for communicating to students how they are to proceed in their learning efforts. There is no ambiguity in how to use the TLU, especially for the most important user—the student.

Danny G. Langdon
Series Editor

PREFACE

The Instructional Design Library provides us all with an opportunity to review familiar designs and explore new vistas. I am pleased to have been able to contribute to the Library and look forward to joining you in sharing its benefits.

My contribution, the Teaching-Learning Unit (TLU), is the result of many years of work by teachers, students, and educational psychologists. Literally thousands have contributed to the development of the Teaching-Learning Unit: The American Institutes for Research, and specifically Dr. John C. Flanagan, the "innovator" behind Project PLAN which gave birth to the TLU; Dr. Robert F. Mager and Dr. William M. Shanner; the AIR staff; teachers and students from participating school districts; and the staff of Westinghouse Learning Corporation devoted much talent to the evolution of the TLU.

I want to express specific thanks to those who assisted in the writing of this book. Dr. William M. Shanner, American Institutes for Research, provided helpful critical comments. Betty Niles, Ithan Elementary School, provided references and assistance with examples for the primary school material. Patricia Forcey, along with Helen Levinstein, of The American College, kept the manuscript moving with typing and editorial assistance. And Howard Hoctor lent his artistic creativity to the Figures.

Most significantly, Danny Langdon, Series Editor, and my colleague at The American College, kept me on track when the light at the end of the tunnel seemed dim.

H.F.R.

CONTENTS

ABSTRACT

THE TEACHING-LEARNING UNIT

The Teaching-Learning Unit (TLU) is an effective document for individualizing instruction. It is a tool to assist a student in assuming responsibility for his or her own learning. The TLU enumerates learning resources and activities to facilitate the accomplishment of specific objectives. The design incorporates existing resources and can be used in a wide range of educational and training settings.

The TLU is a printed document which specifies the intent of instruction, an objective, a self-assessment tool, an example and resources for learning, instructional materials, and activities. It can be used as part of a sophisticated individualized education system as well as in more traditional environments. The TLU can form the backbone of the educational program or can be used on an occasional basis for enrichment or remediation.

THE TEACHING-LEARNING UNIT

I.

USE

The Teaching-Learning Unit is an instructional design developed for the purpose of facilitating individualized instruction. The Teaching-Learning Unit (TLU) was developed as part of Project PLAN (Program for Learning in Accordance with Needs) by the American Institutes for Research under contract from Westinghouse Learning Corporation.* Specifically, the TLU was designed as a tool for student use in a computer managed, individualized instruction system. However, in this book, the focus of the discussion will be on the design and use of the TLU itself, rather than on the function a TLU might fulfill in a computer based education program such as Project PLAN.

The TLU is a tool for individualizing instruction. It is designed to assist a student in assuming responsibility for his or her own learning. It is a guide for students in their use of learning resources. Learning resources are any human or non-human entity that can assist a student in learning. The TLU is normally a consumable document for use by students as a guide for study.

As originally conceived, the TLU was used in kindergarten through twelfth grade. Kindergarten is approaching the lower limit of the use of the document. However, grade twelve is

*The Appendix provides an overview of Project PLAN.

definitely not an upper limit. The basic format of the TLU has been proven useful for students in elementary school, secondary school, colleges, and in adult and continuing education.

The TLU has been used for a considerable range of subject matter, and there is no specific subject matter which can automatically be ruled out. The TLU is a guide for students indicating learning resources to be used and learning activities to be pursued. Therefore, any subject matter in which a student can be presented guidance would be applicable.

The Teaching-Learning Unit is a basic design with a number of possible variations. Originally, in Project PLAN, it was a part of a module. A module was defined as a unit of work requiring approximately two weeks of student effort. Within a module, one or more Teaching-Learning Units would be available. Each Teaching-Learning Unit was designed to speak to a specific set of learner variables. For example, in a module, one TLU might emphasize learning through audio while another might emphasize print.

One of the potential limitations of the Teaching-Learning Unit is the reading ability of students. However, reading can be kept to a minimum by a careful choice of directions on the TLU itself and referencing a minimum of print learning resources. Especially at the lower grade levels, students needed to be able to read or follow specially designed symbols. More detail on the specially designed symbols will be given later in this book. The Design Format section discusses specific modifications made in the TLU design for the purpose of instructing primary school students.

Two basic designs exist for the Teaching-Learning Unit. These are the *materials-general* Teaching-Learning Unit and the *materials-specific* Teaching-Learning Unit. The specification of each design will be given later. However, at this point a general indication of their use will be given.

The *materials-specific* Teaching-Learning Unit consists of four basic parts:
1. objective
2. example
3. materials list
4. activity list

The *materials-specific* TLU points out specific learning resources to be used in accomplishing an objective. In the case of printed material, the specification would be in terms of the specific sections of a book or pamphlet to be used.

The *materials-specific* TLU also illustrates one of the major positive aspects of the TLU. It is designed to make use of existing, and in most cases, commercially available materials. It is not a design that requires teachers to construct a totally new curriculum, or learning materials from scratch. Any specific resources, such as books, films, kits, people, etc., can be specified as resources to use in a *materials-specific* TLU.

In contrast, the *materials-general* TLU consists of five basic parts. As in the *materials-specific* TLU, the *materials-general* TLU begins with objectives and an example. Three unique parts of this TLU are: learning activities, key words, and specific resources. In total the five parts of the *materials-general* TLU are:
1. objective
2. example
3. learning activities
4. key words
5. specific resources

No specific materials are pointed out in a *materials-general* TLU. Rather, generalizations are given so that students may know where to find materials that would be useful.

The *materials-general* Teaching-Learning Unit has three salient features. First, as a learning tool it can act as a challenge for students and as a tool in helping them learn to become more actively involved in their own learning. As students use a *materials-general* TLU, they are able to adapt the resources available to them to their specific learning styles. Second, the *materials-general* TLU can be used to evaluate a student's capability to locate and use learning resources. A *materials-general* TLU completed by a student provides a record of the manner in which the learning problem was attacked. By periodically using this type of TLU, it is possible to monitor the progress of a student as a learner, irrespective of the subject matter being used. Third, administratively the *materials-general* TLU is a highly adaptable design. Since it does not specify materials, it can be used with almost any learning materials. If students are not capable of operating on their own with a *materials-general* TLU, the instructor or other students can use this unit as a guide, indicating to the students where they might find useful materials. A *materials-general* TLU completed by a student becomes a valuable tool for use by other students independently or in peer tutoring.

It was mentioned at the outset that the TLU was originally developed to be part of Project PLAN, an individualized instruction system. While the TLU can be used as part of a very formal system of instruction, it also can be used in a number of other ways. The TLU can be used in a system of instruction that is less formal than Project PLAN, yet is systematized. Having a set of TLUs covering a curriculum would enable an instructor to build an individualized instruction system without the aid of a computer. Of course, without a properly designed computer system, the logistics of the system can be overpowering—and some efficient administrative system, such as using paraprofessionals for assistance, should be devised.

The TLU can be used effectively apart from a completely individualized instructional system. For example, students who are in a group instructional situation and need special remedial help, practice, or review can be referred to a TLU. Likewise, a TLU can be a special resource for independent study and, as such, can be built into other instructional designs, as either preparatory or post-classroom instruction study.

II.

OPERATIONAL DESCRIPTION

The Teaching-Learning Unit is an instructional design developed for the purpose of facilitating individualized instruction. It may be used by a teacher to individualize a very small segment of a total course, or it may be incorporated as part of a major individualized instruction system, such as Project PLAN. A detailed description of the use of TLUs in major systems of individualized education is beyond the scope of this book. The remainder of this chapter is devoted to the use of TLUs to facilitate the individualization of instruction in a setting which is not part of a major individualized instructional effort.

Consider a situation in which a teacher is conducting a classroom in a normal group mode of instruction. A test is given to the total class. In analyzing the results of the test, the teacher determines that a small number of students need additional remedial work on a few objectives, but that the majority of the class is ready to move on. From a student's and teacher's perspective, let's examine how the TLU design might be of assistance in this situation.

A limited number of objectives have been noted to be causing difficulty for a few students. Two possibilities exist with respect to TLUs. First, TLUs may be available covering these materials, or they may not. If a TLU is available covering the objectives that need remedial work, it can be assigned to a student to do either at a study time in class or as out-of-class work. The student's activities will be examined in more detail shortly.

Suppose that a TLU does not exist covering the objectives on which the students need remedial work. Here again the teacher has two choices. One choice is to meet with each student and orally describe to the student the activities that should be undertaken in order to accomplish the necessary remedial learning. The other alternative is to develop a TLU for use by the student. In most cases the preferable alternative is to develop a TLU for use by the student.

The objective for the TLU already exists, since it is presumed to have been the basis upon which the test just given was developed. An example may not already exist, but probably can be derived quickly from the test items used in the test. This leaves the teacher with only two parts of a TLU to complete: a materials list and an activity list.

Drawing upon his or her knowledge of existing resources and also taking into consideration the student's particular difficulty, it is not too difficult for the teacher to list materials that a student might use in remedial study and also enumerate the activities in which a student might engage to accomplish an objective. It is also possible that the teacher could develop a *materials-general* TLU and leave the specific learning resource specification to the student. More detail on TLU development is provided in the Developmental Guide section of this book.

Once a TLU exists, it can be handed out, and the student can proceed with study. The student uses the objective, example, and remainder of the TLU for study. Of course, the teacher is always available to provide assistance. Not only does the TLU provide guidance for the student's learning, but it also provides a reference that the student can fall back on for later review.

Upon completion of the TLU, the student would show it to the teacher. It is desirable that the student and the teacher have a dialogue to determine how successful the TLU was in meeting the student's needs. If improvements could be made in the TLU, that should be noted in a file by the teacher for future use. If the TLU being used by the student is one that has just been developed, it should be put in a permanent file for future reference. This way, even though a teacher begins with a very limited number of TLUs, a file can continually be augmented until a wealth of resources is available. Most of us are impatient and would like to have a complete file of TLUs or other learning resources available instantaneously. In most cases, such a wish is just not practical. We can, however, by careful planning, develop over a period of years a rich resource for ourselves as well as for our colleagues.

Let's look in greater detail into how a student who has been assigned a TLU would work through it.

Materials-Specific TLU

As noted earlier, the *materials-specific* Teaching-Learning Unit has four basic components:
1. objective
2. example
3. material list
4. activity list

Figure 1 outlines the flow of student activity (see figure on next page).

Using a TLU the student first reads the objective to be accomplished. Then, the student reads the example following the objective. In a sense, the example can be thought of as a test item or an operational definition of the objective, which provides the student with a self-check. For instance, the objective might be: "Be able to find the sum of two whole numbers." An example for the objective could be "Find the

Figure 1

Materials-Specific TLU

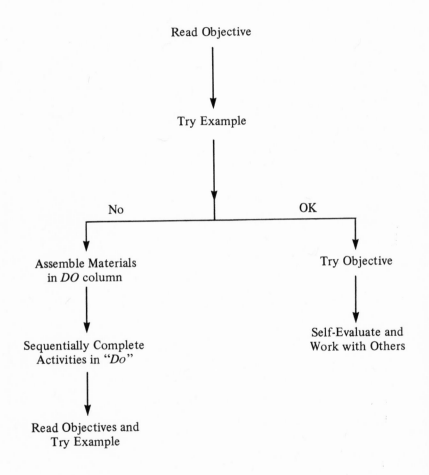

sum of 18 and 21." A file of correct responses or criteria for evaluating an example can be kept by the instructor. The openness with which these answers are available to the students will depend upon their maturity. If students feel their primary goal is to get "the answer" to the example, then the items must be kept relatively secure. Although it sounds trite, the student is only cheating himself when he attempts to learn the answer to the example without actually trying it. One of the primary rationales for an example is to provide assistance to the student, to save the student time, and to make the student more efficient in learning. If the student subverts the system, he or she will save time now by not going to the Learning Activities, but will not be prepared for subsequent evaluation and will become frustrated at that time. Let us look more closely at the rationale behind providing an example test item.

Because one-item tests are generally not a reliable means for assessing the achievement of an objective, the student reasons as follows: "If I cannot do what the example asks, then I can be quite certain I cannot perform the objective. Since I cannot perform the objective, I had better concentrate on the learning activities. On the other hand, if I can do what the example asks, I should give some consideration to whether or not I am already able to perform the objective. I could do this in a number of ways. If I am clever, I might make up a number of other problems related to the objective and see if I can solve those." Following the instance above, the student might try finding the sum of 23 and 19 or of 56 and 109. "I might quickly review the activities in the DO COLUMN without taking a great deal of time on them and then check with my fellow students or my teacher to see if it is felt that I can actually perform the objective." The DO COLUMN is the location of the activity list. It will be explained in more detail later. It can be seen from Figure 1 that if the student does well on the example, this is not the end of the line. This student should carefully work with himself or herself, as well as with other students and possibly the instructor, to review alternate forms of examples for the objective. Often a short conference with the instructor will suffice to assist the student in validating or invalidating his or her perception of performance on the example. The essence of the objective and the example is twofold; (1) to provide a student with an indication of what is to be achieved, and (2) to provide him or her a means for preliminary self assessment.

Assuming a student does, in fact, need to work on the learning activities, the next step in the *materials-specific* TLU would be to collect the required resources from the classroom, library, or wherever they might be found. It is important in designing the TLU that the materials listed in the USE COLUMN be listed in a consistent fashion so that students can use this document as a quick and easy reference in locating materials. The USE COLUMN is the location of the materials list and will be discussed in detail later.

Because students must locate their own materials, the classroom or resource center must be arranged in such a way that it is accessible to students. Part of the value of using a TLU is to encourage students to develop their reference skills. That is, students are not merely handed a book and told to turn to page 35. Rather, they are told that materials are contained in a book, on page 35, and they have to *locate* that book and bring it to their desk or work station for use. Operating this type of classroom necessitates mobility on the part of students, encourages student responsibility, and enhances interpersonal skills.

With the instructional materials in hand, the student's attention is turned to the DO COLUMN. This column of the TLU lists activities which a student should do, using the instructional materials listed in the USE COLUMN to achieve an objective. Thus, if the USE COLUMN indicates students should read pages 645 to 651 of a textbook, the student would then read those pages. Following instructions to read, there might also be directions asking the student to answer specific questions, which he or she would then do. All activities should be included in the TLU for a specific purpose. In most instances that purpose relates specifically to the accomplishment of the objective seen in the TLU. In other instances, activities designed to assist the student in accomplishing longer-range objectives, for example, developing time management skills, are deliberately included.

Although it is not essential in most cases, students will work through the material in the DO COLUMN in a linear order. If a specific sequencing is a necessity, that information should be clearly communicated to the student. On the other hand, if the order is merely a suggested sequence, the student should do all the activities, but may not need to do them in the order specified. When students are reviewing the items contained in the DO COLUMN, in conjunction with the materials specified in the USE COLUMN, they may need to engage in some scheduling activities. For example, if a student must use a video cassette player, it is likely that the student will have to schedule the use of that equipment, either formally or informally. As a student is preparing to work on the TLU, he or she should make note of the fact that a piece of equipment is needed, and then schedule it appropriately.

It should be obvious by now that the TLU is a procedural guide that handles many of the necessary procedures in a teacher-led classroom. Teachers do not have to say, "open your books to page 35," but rather can rely on the TLU to provide that direction. Likewise, the mechanical flow through the learning activities does not have to be continuously directed and monitored by the teacher.

After the student has worked through all the learning activities for a specific objective, he or she then returns to the beginning of the TLU, and again reads the objective and the example. At this point, the student should feel comfortable that he or she can, in fact, do what the example asks and can perform the behavior specified in the objective. If the student has conscientiously completed all the learning activities, and still does not feel confident, the problems should be discussed with the teacher. The teacher may wish then to assign other activities. On the other hand, if a student feels comfortable that he or she can accomplish the objective, the student would proceed through the other objectives of the Teaching-Learning Unit. When the student has come to an appropriate stopping point at the end of the TLU, he or she would review all objectives and might take an appropriate test. Again, it should be emphasized that the testing in not an integral feature of the TLU design, but rather a component of a larger instructional system. However, I would recommend that in the use of TLU some provision be made for assessment of student competency.

Materials-General TLU

To review the components of the *materials-general* TLU, they are:
1. objective
2. example
3. learning activities
4. key words
5. specific resources

Figure 2 outlines the flow of student activity (see next page).

The student begins work on the *materials-general* TLU in the same manner he or she would begin in the *materials-specific* design. The student reads the objective, attempts the example, and through the process described above, deter-

Figure 2

Materials-General TLU

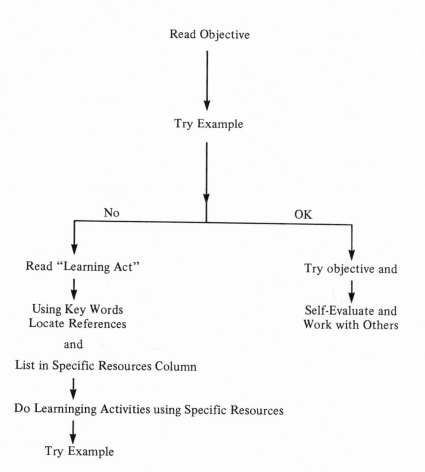

Read Objective

Try Example

No   OK

Read "Learning Act"   Try objective and

Using Key Words   Self-Evaluate and
Locate References   Work with Others

and

List in Specific Resources Column

Do Learninging Activities using Specific Resources

Try Example

mines whether or not it is appropriate to continue through the learning activities.

The *materials-general* TLU is a more generic document, allowing for greater flexibility in the classroom and demanding more sophisticated learning skills on the part of the student. The learning activities indicate the tasks in which a student should engage, but not specify any particular resources to be used. Students must therefore develop some way in which to determine what specific learning materials to use in order to achieve the objective. This is learned from the use of materials-specific TLUs in the past, or from a general self-sophistication in study methodology by the student. In addition, students may ask other students or their teacher for assistance in locating materials. However, the point of the learning activities is to define work which contributes to the accomplishment of the objective. In essence, the student should be provided with a series of activities which, when accomplished completely, will lead to the mastery of the objective.

For example, a learning activity related to the understanding of early American history might ask the student to read the Declaration of Independence. In the materials-general TLU, the student would not be given a specific resource but would be told to read the Declaration of Independence. Based on prior knowledge, the student might know that this document could be found in a textbook in the classroom, in a reference book in the library, or possibly in some pamphlets contained in a special section of the library. The main point is that the student knows what activities must be accomplished but must exercise independence in determining and locating the specific resources utilized.

To assist the student in accomplishing the learning activities, two other resources are needed: key words and specific resources. Key words or guide words provide a student with assistance in locating specific reference resources. These words might be used by the student in accessing the card catalogue of a library or using the index of books. To continue our example, if the student has been asked to read the Declaration of Independence, key words might be "Declaration of Independence," "Independence," "Jefferson," "Philadelphia, 1776." These words provide the student with some assistance on where to begin to look in order to find appropriate material.

Specific resources are not specified by the designer of the *materials-general* TLU. The learner must seek and locate the specific resources to be used in carrying out the learning activities. Once the student has determined specific resources and has performed the learning activities for the TLU, he or she has put together a valuable resource guide for review in future study. It is a truism that no one learns a subject well until they have to teach it, and in part the materials-general TLU is designed to help the student be his or her own teacher.

As an aside, it can be beneficial to the instructor to compile the specific resources developed by students. These resources can then be used in developing *materials-specific* TLUs. Also, a *materials-general* TLU developed by one student may then be used by another student on an alternative format of a *materials-specific* TLU.

As mentioned earlier, the *materials-general* TLU can be thought of as a very flexible document to be used with a variety of resources, many of which may not be known to the writer of the TLU ahead of time. A teacher may fill in a portion of the specific resources column before giving the *materials-general* TLU to the student. If a teacher knows of specific, important resources in the learning environment, and wishes to call these to the student's attention, it can be written into the specific resources column. Using the *materials-general* TLU, there is an unlimited variety of resources that can be developed for student use.

Specific mention should be made of the role of the teacher in the effective use of TLUs. When TLUs are in use, the teacher is no longer the procedural "traffic cop" of the learning environment. The teacher's main role is to diagnose student difficulties, guide the students into appropriate learning activities, and clarify concepts which are difficult. The teacher works with individual students or groups of students; but, for the most part, not with a class as a whole. The role of the teacher in the learning environment is not unlike that of other resources.

In summary, operationally the TLU is used to facilitate individualized learning. By adding TLUs to a file, it is possible for a teacher to develop a very rich resource over a relatively short period of time. This resource can be revised continually and drawn upon to individualize student learning.

III.

DESIGN FORMAT

During the early developmental efforts on Project PLAN, a number of different designs were considered and used for the Teaching-Learning Unit.

This chapter will describe three different types of TLUs. First, a *materials-specific* TLU to be used with higher grades and adults; second, a *materials-general* TLU for the same audience; and, finally, a TLU to be used with primary school students. The description of the design format is intended to be useful to the instructor who wishes to develop TLUs for use by himself or herself and others. It is not the intent of these descriptions to replicate in detail the features of the TLU as used in the original Project PLAN or in PLAN as is currently offered by Westinghouse Learning Corporation.

A basic principle of the TLU is that it should be *brief*. It uses concise wording, and it directs the student to learning resources. It is a cueing device and not a literary document. The designer must resist the temptation to become a text author, at least within the confines of the TLU. The TLU can be thought of as a road map for learning; it points the way.

Materials-Specific TLU

This TLU can be designed and used for upper elementary school students, secondary school students, and college

students and adults. The description which follows gives
generalities which would need to be tailored by each writer
to a specific student population. The example comes from
the content area of economics and is based on an economics
course offered by The American College. Figure 3 is used as
a reference throughout this description. You should at this
time carefully peruse the layout illustrated in Figure 3 and
again as the description which follows unfolds.

The *materials-specific* TLU has four basic components:
1. objective
2. example
3. materials list—USE
4. activity list—DO

All four components are designed to work together; however,
from a student's point of view, the objective and example
bear a close relationship, as do the materials and activities
USE and DO Columns.

At the beginning of the TLU, there is an objective in which
a clear statement is given of the intent of the instruction.
This statement communicates to the student that which is to
be learned, and also provides the initial orientation of the student to the learning activity he or she will undertake. The
objective can also be used as an evaluation tool. As part of an
overall curriculum or system of instruction, the objective
must also have integrity. That is, the objective, as seen on the
TLU, must make sense in itself and must be a device which
can be used in communication with students, other teachers,
and interested parties.

In Figure 3, the objective has been drawn from an economics curriculum. Standing alone, the objective has integrity. In addition, the objective is an integral part of a
section of economics study defined as International Trade
and Economic Growth. The objective should be worthwhile
in itself and should contribute to a broader understanding

Figure 3

A Materials Specific TLU

Objective: Distinguish between the gold standard and a system of floating (flexible) exchange rates in terms of:

    a. how the foreign exchange rate is determined
    b. how equilibrium in international trade is determined
    c. the effect of a change in domestic price on equilibrium

EXAMPLE:

Which of the following statements correctly explain how equilibrium in in international trade is achieved (determined) under a system of "flexible (floating) exchange rates"?

   I. If the foreign exchange rate rises, foreign goods become more costly in relation to domestic goods, exports tend to increase and imports tend to decrease.

   II. Equilibrium is achieved by government restricting changes in rates to the predetermined range or "bands" specified in response to devaluations initiated by foreign countries.

   III. Changes in foreign exchange rates represent real changes in relative prices, thereby causing exports and imports to respond by changing to seek a new equilibrium level.

   IV. The gold-flow, price-level adjustment mechanism provides a new equilibrium in response to gold movements.

   V. Government assures equilibrium by initiating devaluation
     . . . A.   I and II only
     . . . B.   I and III only
     . . . C.   II and IV only
     . . . D.   I, III, and V only
     . . . E.   I, II, III, and IV only

(continued on next page)

Figure 3
(continued)

USE	DO
The Money Exchange (1976). The American College, Bryn Mawr, Pa. 3/4" Video Cassette.	(a) View the tape to gain an view of the topic
Samuelson, Paul H. *Economics* Tenth Edition. McGraw-Hill, 1976.	(b) Read Pages 645-651
The Money Exchange (1976). The American College, Bryn Mawr, Pa. 3/4" Video Cassette.	(c) Review the section of the tape titled Exchange Rates
The Money Exchange (1976). The American College, Bryn Mawr, Pa. Summary Sheet.	(d) Study the material on Hume's Mechanism

Using all of the above resources restate

(e) In your own words the information necessary to complete this chart on a full sized sheet of paper (save for review):

	Gold Standard	Floating Exchange Rates
How the foreign exchange rate is determined		
How equilibrium in international trade is determined		
The effect on equilibrium of a change in domestic price		

of the concepts contained in the area of study known as International Trade and Economic Growth.

The second component of the *materials-specific* TLU is the example. This looks very much like a test question and, in fact, is one. Logically one could ask why the example is not called a test item or sample test item, rather than muddying the water by using the term example. In some early work done in Project PLAN, it was found that students misinterpreted the intent of the example when it was called a test item or sample test item. Students didn't seem to be able to shed themselves of the idea that this was one of the test items they would see in a later examination. In some cases this was true; however, in the vast majority of cases, the specific example used in the TLU was not replicated verbatim on a test for students. To avoid confusion and communicate precisely the intent of this component of the TLU, the term example was adopted.

The example serves at least three purposes which should be kept in mind in the design of a TLU. The example serves to clarify the objective. In theory a student should understand an objective when it is read. However, in practice, it is often useful to attempt to communicate the objective to the student in alternate ways. Providing an example often operationalizes the objective in terms a student can more readily understand. Second, the example is used as a self-check for the student. If the student attempts the example and is not successful, it is clear that the student has not mastered the objective and needs additional work. On the other hand, if the student attempts the example and is successful, this is an indication that the student may have already mastered the objective and, therefore, may not need to spend time on it. Students have to be cautioned at first, but eventually they do develop a healthy skepticism for testing themselves with one example.

For some objectives there is only one valid example and one valid test item. In this case, if the student can do what the example asks, he knows he can perform the objective. For example, if a student has an objective of running the 100 yard dash in 11 seconds or less, the example would ask the student to run the 100 yards, and the student would know the criteria for success was being able to perform the activity in 11 seconds or less. It would be clear to the student from having performed the one example whether or not he had, in fact, accomplished the objective. On the other hand, in the area of mathematics, if the student had an objective of being able to add any two numbers, there is an infinite number of possible test questions that could be asked. If the student can perform just one or two examples, this is not adequate. The student would need to test himself quite thoroughly to be sure that the objective had been mastered.

A third rationale for the inclusion of an example is to indicate to the student how the evaluation would be carried out. The example does not give the precise question that will be asked on an examination, but it does give the student an indication of the manner in which the evaluation will be carried out. In Figure 3, the example serves the purpose of indicating how the student will be evaluated on the objective, as well as providing the student with opportunity for self-check.

The objective and example work together to provide the student with an overview of the material to be mastered and a mechanism for self-evaluation.

The materials list area is the third component of the TLU, and is identified in the format by the heading, "USE." The USE COLUMN specifies the instructional material that the student will use in studying, and the DO COLUMN indicates what the student will actually do with these materials. (The specifics will be described later in this chapter.) The

detail with which it is necessary to spell out activities in the
USE and DO COLUMNS varies with the level of sophistication of student study skills. Because the TLU is used in an
individualized instruction setting, even mature college students or adults may need some time to become appropriately
oriented to this mode of instruction.

The USE COLUMN is a resource inventory enumerating
for the students the materials that are necessary for use in
study. It is in many ways a mechanical communications system to present vital information to the student without the
necessity of an instructor presenting this information indi-
vidually to each student. Once a student has a TLU, the
material to be used is known and the student can continually
go back to that reference source without consulting the
teacher. In the development of the TLU, the materials that
are listed in the USE COLUMN provide alternatives for
study. Referring to Figure 3, it can be noted that three
separate materials are used in this TLU: a text book, a video-
cassette, and a printed summary sheet.

Let's consider some alternative to the USE COLUMN.
There are numerous textbooks available on the subject of
economics which could be used by students in accomplishing this objective. Instead of referencing the Samuelson text,
the developer of the TLU could have referenced any number
of other textbooks which might meet the needs of students.
The alternate textbooks might be more appropriate for
certain students, depending upon their reading level, their
fields of interest, or for a variety of other reasons. Suppose
the students are highly quantitatively oriented, for example,
a group of engineers taking economics. It would be desirable
to use a text which is highly quantitative in its approach to
economics. On the other hand, if the students are a group of
fine arts students who are relatively unsophisticated in quantitative techniques, a textbook employing a less quantitative

approach would be more appropriate. With reference to the videotape, the developer of the TLU may not have access to this tape, but may know of a good film, filmstrip, or audio-tape in a resource collection. In developing the TLU, the developer would rely on the resources available. It should be noted that specific TLUs can be tailored to perceived or known learning styles of a group. If it were desirable to develop a TLU with a high audio orientation for students with very poor reading skills the USE COLUMN could contain a heavy dose of audio or visual materials and could be very sparse in printed material. On the other hand, if the group toward which the material is being oriented is highly sophisticated with respect to their reading and comprehension skills (many business executives would fall into this category), printed materials which are highly condensed would be appropriate.

The fourth column of the *materials-specific* TLU is an activity list, and is identified in the format by the heading, "DO." This column specifies the manner in which the student will interact with instructional materials. The primary purpose for the DO COLUMN is to communicate to the student the activities he or she will engage in during learning.

The items in the DO COLUMN are listed in the sequence in which the designer feels the student should go through the material. It is virtually impossible to be *certain* that a student will go through the material in the order specified. However, it is *likely* that students will go through material in the order presented. In many cases it is desirable to communicate to the student whether or not it is thought to be best to go through the material in the order specified or whether the order is insignificant. This can be done by establishing some type of convention within your instructional setting or by merely noting in the DO COLUMN a few words saying, "order is important" or "order is unimportant." Indicating the latter to students is beneficial. First, some students like to arrange their own learning, and know approaches which work best for them. It is desirable to allow such students to proceed in a manner they think is best. Only in cases of strict prerequisites would the instructor want to caution the student about proceeding in an alternate fashion.

As an example, in Figure 3 the student is asked to first view the videotape to gain an overview of the subject matter and then read the materials in Samuelson. There is no prerequisite in this order and, therefore, there would be no reason that a student could not read the material and then view the videotape. Consider in contrast a chemistry experiment in which the order of activities in important. A good rule of thumb is to not imply or impose a specific order unless it is absolutely necessary. By modifying the order of activities presented in the TLU, it is possible to suggest to students alternate manners of interacting with instructional materials.

Alternate types of activities that can be included in the DO COLUMN are almost infinite and they do not have to involve activities done independently. For example, the student could be told in Item e of Figure 3 that when he or she had completed filling in the chart, it should be shared with another student who has also completed the chart to discuss areas of discrepancy.

In summary, the USE and DO COLUMN work together to provide the student with a road map to follow for learning as the student works through the materials in the DO COLUMN. He or she can constantly refer to the objective and the example to ascertain progress toward the final goal.

Materials-General TLU

The *materials-general* TLU is much more flexible in design but requires a more mature learner. The first two components of the *materials-general* TLU are the same as for the *materials-specific* TLU. These are the objective and the example. The other three components of the *materials-general* TLU are: learning activities, key words, and specific resources. Figure 4 illustrates this type of TLU.

Learning activities are those tasks the student should undertake in order to accomplish the objective. These are normally provided in the order in which the student should undertake them. The student is told what activities to do but not told the specific resources to use. In this respect the name given to the TLU is very descriptive. It is general with respect to materials, but specific with respect to learning activities to be carried out.

In Figure 4, the first learning activity, labeled (a), illustrates the generality of this TLU. The learning activity indicates the student should study the material on a specific content area, but does not specify the specific resources. A student may turn to text material, films, records, audiotapes, or whatever resource is available in the learning environment. The primary requirement for including an item in the learning activities column is that it focusses directly on the objective. Learning activities are selected to lead to the achievement of the objective. In theory, sophisticated learners should not need to have learning activities specified. Rather, they should be able to look at the objective and derive the learning activities necessary to accomplish that objective. However, the *materials-general* TLU takes one step back from that ideal and provides guidance for the student in the type of activities that might be undertaken in order to accomplish the objective.

Item (b) in the learning activities column of Figure 4 illustrates a rather focussed activity, whereas (a) does not. Different students' interpretations of the term "study" as contained in (a) might vary. However, the interpretation of

Figure 4

A Materials-General TLU

Objective: Distinguish between the gold standard and a system of floating (flexible) exchange rates in terms of:

    a. how the foreign exchange rate is determined
    b. how equilibrium in international trade is determined
    c. the effect of a change in domestic price on equilibrium

EXAMPLE:

Which of the following statements correctly explain how equilibrium in international trade is achieved (determined) under a system of "flexible (floating) exchange rates"?

    I. If the foreign exchange rate rises, foreign goods become more costly in relation to domestic goods, exports tend to increase and imports tend to decrease.

    II. Equilibrium is achieved by government restricting changes in rates to the predetermined range or "bands" specified in response to devaluations initiated by foreign countries.

    III. Changes in foreign exchange rates represent real changes in relative prices, thereby causing exports and imports to respond by changing to seek a new equilibrium level.

    IV. The gold-flow, price-level adjustment mechanism provides a new equilibrium in response to gold movements.

    V. Government assures equilibrium by initiating devaluation when necessary.

        . . . A.   I and II only
        . . . B.   I and III only
        . . . C.   II and IV only
        . . . D.   I, III, and V only
        . . . E.   I, II, III, and IV only

(continued on next page)

Figure 4
(continued)

LEARNING ACTIVITIES	KEY WORDS	SPECIFIC RESOURCES
(a) Study general material on the gold standard and floating (flexible) exchange rates with particular emphasis on a, b, and c of the objective.	gold standard flexible exchange rates floating exchange rates equilibirum domestic price foreign exchange Hume mechanism	
(b) Write a definition for: gold standard; floating (flexible) exchange rates; foreign exchange rate; equilibrium in international trade.		
(c) For each of a, b, and c of the objective write a statement in terms of the gold standard and in terms of floating exchange rates. Compare your definition with one done by a fellow student.		

"write a definition," as in activity (b), is more precise. In the learning activities column of the materials-general TLU, it is possible to vary the range of specificity with respect to learning activities themselves.

Item (c) in the learning activities column of Figure 4 illustrates an important point in TLU design. A similar point is illustrated in Item (e) in the DO COLUMN of the materials-specific TLU shown in Figure 3. Both of these activities call for a summary or culminating activity on the part of the student. The student is directed to do an activity which brings together all parts of the objective. A common error in developing TLUs, or for that matter many other types of instruction, is to provide the student with an opportunity to practice the specific pieces of an objective, but not put it all together. Thus, even though the student is writing definitions in (b) and might be assumed to know how to do the entire objective, activity (c) brings it all together. It should be noted that in (c) the student is directed to work with another student to check his or her definition. The rationale for this is twofold. First, from the point of view of accomplishing this specific objective, it is desirable for students to be able to check their work. Second, this item provides an opportunity for meaningful interaction. With this in mind, we are now ready to turn our attention to the fourth section of the *materials-general* TLU—the key word column.

The key word column indicates key words or phrases a student could use to locate appropriate reference material to be used in conjunction with the learning activities. It is not a location for vocabulary words. If a student is expected to know how to define, use, etc., specific terms, this information should be conveyed in the learning activities column. In the key word column the only intent is to provide an enumeration of descriptors to be used in locating appropriate material. In many cases the list will go well beyond the vocabulary needs of the student. As can be seen in Figure 4, both the terms "flexible exchange rate" and "floating exchange rate" are used. The terms "flexible" and "floating" can be used interchangeably, but some authors use one term and some another. If a student is provided with both, it is more likely he or she will locate appropriate resources.

Words included in the key words column are often obvious terms that could be derived by the most naive student. In the example of Figure 4, you will note that many of the terms come directly from the objective. This is repetitious, but does serve to call attention to the appropriate key phrases in the objective. In part, then, it can be said that one reason for the key word column is to assist students in learning how to intelligently read objectives. The last entry in the key words column in Figure 4, "Hume mechanism," illustrates another important feature of this component. Nowhere in the objective is the term "Hume mechanism" found. The writer of the TLU knew, however, that material related to the objective could be found in material on the "Hume mechanism." Therefore, a useful key term is included for the student, one that cannot be derived even by a close scrutinization of the objective itself.

Finally, the fifth and final section of the *materials-general* TLU is the specific resources column. This column is left blank, and that makes it easy for the instructional designer. The blank space is left for the convenience of the student. In this column the student places specific resources that can be used for the accomplishment of the objective. In essence, the learning activities and key words are used as inputs, and the specific resources as an output. When this has been done, the student has constructed his or her own version of a *materials-specific* TLU with the specific materials now specified and the associated learning activities.

Once a student has filled in the learning resources column, he or she has a valuable tool for study, one which has been developed to meet his or her own learning needs. In some cases, the instructor will need to work very closely with the student, especially on an initial basis in locating appropriate materials for inclusion in the learning resources column. Obviously, new and pertinent materials found by students and noted by the teacher can become valuable sources for the teacher in current and future planning activities for improving learning effectiveness.

In summary, the *materials-general* TLU is a highly flexible tool enabling the instructor to provide guidance for learning in a wide variety of environments. It has as an additional advantage: the flexibility of being updated to take into account the very latest in learning resources, even those published after the TLU was originally developed.

Primary School TLU

The teaching-learning unit design for primary students has many of the same features as for secondary and higher level students. However, a number of modifications have been made in order to make it more useful to young children. These modifications, in many ways, alleviate the problems students might have in reading and managing their own learning. There is not an arbitrary grade level or chronological time when students should be switched from primary type TLUs to the secondary and higher level designs shown earlier. The shift is in emphasis rather than in design and should be made gradually. In this book, examples are used from the diverse ends of the educational spectrum. Figure 5 is a primary level TLU to be used by preschool and first grade students. On the other hand, Figures 3 and 4 are teaching-learning units to be used with college-age students and adults. The basic design of the TLU, however, is applicable at these

Figure 5

Primary Level TLU

NAME: ....

	USE	DO	DONE
a	Tape H	Listen	
b	BOOK This Number THREE	Read	
	T INTRODUCE NUMBER RODS FOR ACTIVITY C		
c	Number Rods	Play	
d	Work Book — Pencil Worksheet 8 & 9	Write	8 9 *T*

ends of the range, as well as for the broad number of students in the middle grades. The specifics should be developed based on the teacher's experience with the level of students being considered.

The TLU for the primary level does not have objectives and examples placed at the beginning for student use. This flows from a deliberate decision made in the early development of Project PLAN. Objectives were placed at the end of a TLU and were for the *teachers'* use. In Figure 5 objectives are not actually shown, and neither is an example. Points for self-check and teacher-check can be seen.

The primary TLU is divided into smaller segments than higher level TLUs. These smaller blocks of work are designed to assist the students in developing a management system for their own learning and to enable them to have a sense of accomplishment in completing relatively short units of work. In Figure 5 it can be seen that lines and boxes are drawn on the TLU in contrast to the more open layout of the other TLUs. This design enables students to focus more closely on the work they are pursuing.

The primary TLU is a materials-specific TLU. The specific materials used, as well as what the student is to do with them, are spelled out.

The USE section is designed to tell students what they are to use in their work. It can be seen in Figure 5 that for activity "a," a tape is needed; activity "b," a book; activity "c," number rods; and for activity "d," a workbook and pencil. Students begin their work on any activity by gathering the materials in the USE COLUMN.

Symbols, as well as words, are used in the primary TLU to assist students in locating materials. In the USE COLUMN of Figure 5, five different symbols are used. These are for a tape, book, number rods, workbook, and a pencil. The symbols for the tape, book, and workbook are generic and would

be used in a variety of locations. For example, if in another
TLU, tape A were used, the same symbol would be presented, but underneath the tape it would say tape A rather
than tape H. The same symbol is used in a number of TLUs.
It is important that both the picture and word be included
rather than only the picture. As a student's vocabulary develops it is desirable to gradually withdraw the picture and use
only the words. Caution should be exercised in developing an
over-reliance in the symbols on the part of the student.

The pencil symbol in activity "d" is generic and would be
used over and over. The "T" indicates the need for the student to check with the teacher. But the number rods symbol
in "c" is specific to a particular manipulative device.

In setting up materials for use in primary TLUs, great care
must be taken to label the materials and convey the exact
meaning of the labeling effectively. Students also must know
where the various materials can be found, particularly if they
are materials used by a large number of students. Classroom
organization is very important.

The DO COLUMN provides information to the students
on what they are to do with the materials found in the USE
COLUMN. Again, symbols are used to convey information.
In the DO COLUMN, indications are made when a student
should work with other students, or check with the teacher.
In activity "c" it can be seen that the student is to work with
a partner in the use of number rods; and in activity "d,"
the student is to check with the teacher when that activity
is done.

The DONE COLUMN provides the location for students
to check off the activities they have completed, and thus
keep a record of their work. Since it is likely that a student
will not complete an entire TLU in one continuous time
period, it is important for the student to have a place to indicate what work has been completed. In using the TLU, the

student would place a check mark in the DONE COLUMN after completing that activity. Thus, after listening to the tape in activity "a," the student would check off the corresponding space in the DONE COLUMN. Activity "d" illustrates another more specific use of the DONE COLUMN. For activity "d," the student is called upon to complete worksheets 8 and 9. When the student has completed worksheet 8, he or she can check that off, and likewise, can check off worksheet 9 when completed. The DO COLUMN in "d" calls for a teacher-check. When the student has completed the activities for "d," he or she checks with the teacher. The teacher can indicate that the activity has been successfully completed in the box in the DONE COLUMN. Although it is expected that teachers will check with students on a regular basis, the teacher-check is a special flag which reminds the students that it is important to check with the teacher before proceeding.

The teacher-line is another feature of the primary TLU. It can be seen between activities "b" and "c" of Figure 5. Students are directed to check with their teacher before proceeding. The purpose of the teacher-line is to provide directions to the teacher, and may in fact refer the teacher to other materials, such as a teacher's manual. In Figure 5, the purpose of the teacher-line is to tell the teacher that it is necessary to introduce the student to the activity involving the number rods. Students know that when they come to a teacher-line it is necessary to check with the teacher before proceeding. While it would be possible for the teacher to figure out what needs to be done without the teacher-line and specific references, in an individualized instruction program, where many students are working on many different materials, it is highly desirable to provide this additional form of management assistance for the teacher.

IV.

OUTCOMES

The Teaching-Learning Unit is a design with considerable flexibility and advantages for both the student and teacher. The majority of these advantages are derived from the characteristics of individualized instruction and are not unique to the use of TLU.

Briefly, some of the advantages of individualized instruction are:

Curriculum Flexibility: From a bank of objectives, the program of study can be developed to meet individual student needs. These needs may be for normal instruction, accelerated or enrichment activity, or for remedial or review work.

Flexibility of Rate: With individualized material each student can proceed at a rate most suited to his or her learning needs. The rate can range from a creep to a gallop. In individualized instruction, time is a variable factor, but level of achievement normally is not.

Learning Style Accommodation: Individualized instruction can make accommodations for individual learning styles and can provide flexibility in varying learning strategies. Materials can be used to emphasize audio, visual, or print. The level of difficulty or sophistication can be varied in each. The amount of practice needed to accomplish an objective can be varied; likewise, the amount of group interaction, or the degree of independence allowed the student.

Student Responsibility Development: Within a specific resource, such as the TLU, the amount of responsibility placed on the student for self-control of learning can be varied. The materials-specific and materials-general TLUs have provided examples. In addition, the overall program of studies of a student can be developed to promote a gradual, but systematic development of responsibility for self-management of learning.

Turning more specifically to the TLU, students have the advantage of a learning tool which enables them to individualize their own learning and develop their study skills. The students are involved in the responsibility for their own learning. The students may move at their own pace and do not have to continually turn to the teacher for further directions. If TLUs are utilized with the same student population over an extended period of time, they can be designed in such a way that students are continually given more responsibility for their own learning. In this way, students not only learn the content contained in the TLU, but also learn to manage their own instructional time, and develop better study habits. Earlier it was pointed out that the *materials-general* TLU can be used to assess a student's sophistication in organizing his or her own learning.

The TLU is a management tool. As such, it allows the teacher considerable flexibility. Because the teacher must write down instructions for students, the clarity of these instructions can be evaluated and improved through continuous use by the students. An important advantage for the teacher is the continuous evaluation of the effectiveness of the Teaching-Learning Unit and the improvement of subsequent versions. In most cases this is not possible in nonindividualized instruction, or at least in instructional systems which do not have a significant element of documentation. Student use of a *materials-general* TLU results in a further benefit to a teacher. Each student developing a *materials-general* TLU has produced a new learning resource that can be used with other students. The teacher resource file is then enhanced.

Earlier in this chapter it was noted that *materials-general* TLUs can be used to assess a student's capability to organize his or her own learning. This information is significant for an individual student, but collectively it can provide a teacher with important information on the sophistication of a group. Suppose a teacher analyzes a number of *materials-general* TLUs for a group and notes that little or no use is being made of a specific resource. For example, students may be ignoring current periodicals from a nearby library. With this knowledge the teacher can work with the group to develop skill in utilizing the periodicals; a new learning resource. The important point is that the deficiency just described was discovered not through a formal testing program of the teacher, but from source material provided by students. Such goal-free evaluation by perceptive teachers can be invaluable; the collection of this data is facilitated by the *materials-general* TLU.

A final advantage for teachers is that they are freed from the routine of direction giving, and are provided more time to actually work with students. The professional competency of a teacher can be more clearly devoted to student learning.

V.

DEVELOPMENTAL GUIDE

The developmental guide for TLUs will be considered in the following order. First, a discussion of *materials-general* TLUs; second, the *materials-specific*; and, third, the primary. This order is used since the development of the *materials-general* TLU is basic to the development of the others.

The initial step in the development of a TLU is the specification of instructional objectives and test items. Numerous books and other instructional materials have been written on this topic. The author recommends that you use your favorite, or you might consider the three resources listed at the close of this chapter.

Cardinal rule of TLU development: Keep it simple! The TLU is a device to communicate directions to students. The simpler those directions, the better.

Materials-General TLU

In developing the *materials-general* TLU, the task is to specify entries in the learning activities column and the key words column. To accomplish this, the following technique is suggested. The developer should write the objective at the top of a piece of paper, and under it divide the paper into two columns. One should be labeled "KNOW" and the other "DO." The task is to then answer the following questions. "What does a student have to know in order to be able to accomplish the objective" and "What does a student need to be able to do in order to accomplish the objective?" These items are enumerated. If the objectives being used are in their formative stage, it may be found that sub-objectives emerge and should be treated separately. However, we will assume that eventually a listing is made of what the students should know and what they should be able to do in order to accomplish the objective. These items are then sequenced appropriately and placed in the learning activities column. The items that the students need to know are usually enumerated in a way that the students either define or in some way indicate that they know the facts or procedures, and the "DO activities" are written so that the students will actually perform these activities. For example, consider a curriculum in biology. If, in order to accomplish an objective, the students need to know the carbon-oxygen cycle, it would be in order to specify that they develop a diagram of the cycle and appropriately label it. Likewise, if an objective required that students be able to use a microscope, it would be appropriate to ask the students to perform an activity using the microscope.

The KEY WORD column is filled in as follows: The developer reviews the objective and the learning activities and develops a list of key words or resource words that the students could use to access material. When in doubt, it is more appropriate to include key words than exclude them. It should be kept in mind that students will use these key words to access materials; and, because different authors index their materials in different ways, the more alternatives available to the students, the better.

Materials-Specific TLU

Turning to the *materials-specific* TLU, the first two steps of developing an objective and an example are identical with the *materials-general* TLU. The other task in developing a *materials-specific* TLU is the development of items for the USE and DO columns. Here it is best but not essential to begin with an already written *materials-general* TLU and an inventory of the specific resources that are available. The resources available and actually used are indicated in the USE column, and the specific activities that the student would carry out are indicated in the DO column.

It has been my experience that some teachers are much more comfortable developing a *materials-specific* TLU first and then proceeding to a *materials-general*. This preference stems from the normal tendency of teachers to think of materials and activities as being synonymous. A teacher thinks of doing page 35 in a book rather than following the train of thought: "My students need practice in solving problems in addition. I know five books that contain appropriate problems, or I could develop a ditto sheet myself. I think I will assign page 35 of the Smith book." The more experienced the teacher, the greater is the tendency to think first of spe-specific resources, ones that have proven effective in the past.

So don't up upset if you prefer to develop a *materials-specific* TLU before a *general*. Just as there are different learning styles in students, there are different developmental styles in developers.

Primary TLU

The development of a primary TLU is very similar. However, some special considerations are necessary. First, it is important to determine the art work or symbols that will be used. Symbols for look, listen, discussion, paper, pencil, workbooks, etc., are often useful. While the specific symbols used in PLAN* are copyrighted, a teacher can get a good idea of things that might be used by examining the literature on the subject.

Following the determination of the symbols, the teacher or developer needs to think through what the students should use and what they should do in order to accomplish the objective. This is done in a manner very similar to that used for developing previously mentioned TLUs. One difference is that the teachers need to use teacher-lines or notes to themselves or other teachers at appropriate points within the TLU. The teachers must also determine where, or how often, they wish to have the student check with them, and put in a teacher-check. The normal tendency in the development of TLUs is for the developer to initially put in too many checks. Teachers find that many students are much more capable of monitoring their own progress than might initially be expected. For a "rule of thumb" it is suggested that, in doubt, a "teacher-check" be put in and later eliminated rather than vice versa.

A Final Note

Ultimately there is only one expert who can determine whether or not the design of a TLU is effective—that is the student. It is imperative that the students be involved in the development of TLUs. This involvement is most obvious in the try-out stage. However, students who are knowledgeable in a subject matter area are often excellent resource persons in designing TLUs for their peers.

References
(DEVELOPMENTAL GUIDE section)

Dillman, C. M. and H. F. Rahmlow. *Writing Instructional Objectives*. Belmont, California: Fearon, 1972.

Mager, R. F. *Preparing Instructional Objectives* (second edition). Belmont, California: Fearon, 1975.

Mager, R. F. *Measuring Instructional Intent*. Belmont, California: Fearon, 1973.

VI.

RESOURCES

PUBLISHED MATERIAL

Flanagan, J. C. Functional Education for the Seventies. *Phi Delta Kappan*, 1967, 1, 27-32.

Flanagan, J. C., W. M. Shanner, H. J. Brudner, and R. W. Marker. An Individualized Instructional System: PLAN*. In H. Talmage (Ed.), *Systems of Individualized Education*. Berkeley: McCutchan Publishing Corporation, 1975.

Weisgerber, R. A (Ed.) *Developmental Efforts in Individualized Learning*. Itasca, Illinois: F. E. Peacock Publishers, Inc., 1971.

OTHER RESOURCES

The American Institutes for Research designed and led the developmental effort for Project PLAN. The files of AIR are a rich resource and many of the staff are capable and willing to provide information:

American Institutes for Research
P.O. Box 1113
Palo Alto, California 94302

Westinghouse Learning Corporation was instrumental in the development of Project PLAN and continues as the organization responsible for PLAN*:

Westinghouse Learning Corporation—PLAN*
770 Lucerne Drive
Sunnyvale, California 94086

The author continues to be deeply involved in research and development activities and would be pleased to act as a resource:

Dr. Harold F. Rahmlow
The American College
270 Bryn Mawr Avenue
Bryn Mawr, Pa., 19010

VII.

APPENDIX 1

Overview of Project PLAN

This appendix describes Project PLAN as it existed in its developmental stages in the time period 1967-70. During that time period the author served as a principal research scientist for the American Institutes for Research, one of the co-developers of Project PLAN. Since 1970, Westinghouse Learning Corporation has assumed complete responsibility for PLAN and has made a number of refinements in the program. If you desire current information on the status of PLAN* (as it is spelled now, with the asterisk), read the materials by Flanagan, Shanner, Brudner, and Marker or consult Westinghouse Learning Corporation directly.

Why Project PLAN?

Project PLAN had its roots in Project Talent. Project Talent, conducted by the American Institutes for Research under the sponsorship of the U.S. Office of Education, included an extensive battery of tests and questionnaires administered to approximately 440,000 students in grades 9 through 12 of a stratified random sample of secondary schools throughout the United States. A major finding of this study was that there existed very large individual differences in knowledge and level of ability among students in the various grades. This strong overlap in knowledge and ability indicated a need for

51

individualization of educational programs. In addition, Project Talent found that many students did not feel that their education was equipping them well for occupations after they left school. These findings indicated the need for both the individualization of educational programs and the individualization of instruction. Follow-up studies on Project Talent continued to be made, and interested readers are advised to search the current literature for details.

Project PLAN Developmental Activities

Project PLAN was a joint developmental effort on the part of the American Institutes for Research, Westinghouse Learning Corporation, and thirteen participating school districts. The acronym PLAN stands for a *P*rogram of *L*earning in *A*ccordance with *N*eeds. The Project was initiated in the spring of 1967. The first year of the project saw the development of materials for grades 1, 5, 9; the second year, grades 2, 6, and 8; the third year, grades 3, 7, and 11; and the fourth year, grades 4, 8, and 12. Thus, over a four-year period, materials were developed for a total 1 through 12 curriculum. The curriculum provided individualization across grades as well as for various stages within each grade. Any student starting at any grade with Project PLAN materials would have the opportunity to continue his education utilizing those materials.

The thirteen participating school districts sent a teacher for each grade level to work with the professional staff of the American Institutes for Research. These teachers worked on the development of materials one year, and returned to their classroom to teach along with a colleague the second year. Thus, in one year a second grade teacher from each of the participating school districts came to Palo Alto, California, to work with the staff on the development of second grade materials. The following year, that teacher returned to the local school district, and along with one other teacher who had not been in Palo Alto, taught Project PLAN. In this way, Project PLAN received the invaluable expertise of experienced classroom teachers along with the talent of AIR's professional staff of educators and psychologists.

Project PLAN Components
The essential components of Project PLAN were:
1. A guidance program
2. A curriculum
3. Evaluation program

All were integrated under a computer managed instruction system and coordinated with a teacher development program.

The guidance program which was formed included vocational information. It was also integrated with the overall computer managed instruction system. A wide variety of curriculum materials were used, with emphasis on commercially available materials. Learning activities and test items for the curriculum were keyed to specific instructional objectives. Project PLAN developed, with the assistance of local school teachers, educational psychologists, and students, a specific program of studies of instructional objectives for a student to master, and monitored the student's progress on the basis of these objectives.

In Conclusion
Far more has been written about Project PLAN than could possibly be included in a single appendix, monograph, or even a series of monographs. The article by Flanagan, Shanner, Brudner, and Marker reports that the American Institutes for Research has compiled a bibliography of over 70 published materials describing the development activities of Project PLAN during 1967-70. Those interested in more detail on the development aspects of Project PLAN are urged

to read the Flanagan article from *Phi Delta Kappan*; the first six chapters of the Weisgerber book; or write to the American Institutes for Research. Information on today's PLAN* is available from Westinghouse Learning Corporation.

VIII.

APPENDIX 2

PLAN*

The body of the text has discussed the Teaching-Learning Unit (TLU) as an instructional design. The intention has been to provide a means for teachers to develop individualized instruction for their own classrooms.

The developmental efforts of Project PLAN formed the basis for the material contained in the body of the text. In contrast, Appendix 2 provides illustrations of TLUs *currently available* in PLAN* as offered by Westinghouse Learning Corporation. The TLUs are an integral part of the PLAN* educational system.

In the body of the text, a limited range of examples of TLUs was provided. By drawing upon the pool of existing TLUs in PLAN*, it is possible here to present the reader with a wider range of illustrations. This broader scope of materials is designed to provide the reader with ideas which can be incorporated into his or her own work as well as to offer insight into the current materials being used in PLAN*.

It can be seen that the various features of the *materials-general* and the *materials-specific* TLU have been used singularly and in combinations in the various TLUs. An extensive use of motivational art can also be seen in the PLAN* TLUs.

Below is an annotated list of the materials contained in this Appendix.

Changing Animals   Science/Grade 1

The TLU begins with a group activity involving the teacher. Extensive use of motivational art provides directions. In Activities 3 and 4, it will be noted that special activity sheets have been developed as part of the TLU. Activity 7 involves the teacher and student in a progress check.

Words That Substitute   Language Arts/Grade 5

Activity 1 utilizes the motivational art as a worksheet. In Activity 2 the student is called upon to carry out an exercise and to check work in the teacher's edition. Activity 4 uses a specially prepared activity sheet which is part of the TLU.

Presenting a Speech   Language Arts/High School

This TLU format combines features of the *materials-general* as well as the *materials-specific* TLU. In Activity B, an evaluation form is presented for the student's use.

Moire Fun   Mathematics/Grade 8

The TLU illustrated here relies very heavily upon activities performed by the student rather than upon textual material. The student is asked to use an encyclopedia but is not referred to a specific encyclopedia.

Introduction to
Algebra of Functions   Mathematics/High School

This TLU combines features of the *materials-general* as well as the *materials-specific* TLU. The examples provide the student with an opportunity for self-evaluation. Within the learning activities, specific provision is made for working with classmates.

The Difference Is the Same   Social Studies/Grade 3

This TLU makes liberal use of a number of media as well as student-teacher interaction. A specially prepared activity sheet is part of the TLU.

OBJECTIVE

Recognize that animals eat, grow, change, move by themselves, and have babies.

Discuss properties of animals. Read **Childcraft, About Animals,** volume 5, pages 8 through 15.

Choose 1 picture.

Let's See the Animals

Write the properties of your animal.

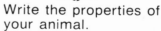

Take turns.

Take a trip to see animals.

Do Activity Sheet 1.

crayons

4

Activity Sheet 2

crayons

pencil

Choose 2 animals.

Watch them for 5 days.
Do Activity Sheet 2.

5

Bring Activity Sheet 2 to the group.

Tell the animals'
properties.

Take turns.

Show the pictures.

6

animal storybook

Read an animal story.

7

Animal Flashcards

Look.

Tell the properties to
your teacher.

3116-1 (5B)

PLAN *Copyright © 1969, 1973 by Westinghouse Learning Corporation. All rights reserved. Authorized for use only with PLAN* Educational System. Printed in U

Check the answers to these questions.

Did you see animals eating? ☐ yes ☐ no

Did you see animals moving? ☐ yes ☐ no

Did you see animal babies? ☐ yes ☐ no

Color a picture of what you saw.

CTIVITY SHEET 2

I chose 2 animals. 1. _____

2. _____

These are their properties.

Animal 1 _____

I watched it on these days _____   _____

_____   _____   _____

Food it eats _____

_____

How it changed _____

_____

_____

How it moved _____

_____

Did it have babies?   ☐   ☐
                       yes   no

Animal 2 _____

I watched it on these days _____ _____

_____ _____ _____

Food it eats _____

_____

How it changed _____

_____

_____

How it moved _____

_____

Did it have babies?   ☐   ☐
                      yes   no

Here are pictures of my animals.

Draw.

3116-1 (7B)

Words That Substitute

OBJECTIVE

Identify and use pronouns correctly.

In the picture above, can you tell which player from the second team will substitute for which player on the first team? Look at the words on the players' shirts and draw a line connecting each player with his substitute.

To learn more about words that substitute for nouns, read the last half of p. 47 and all of p. 48 in *New Directions in English 5*. Do the exercise on p. 48 and check your work in the Teacher's Edition.

Do exercise 3 on p. 191 of *New Directions in English 5*, either in your head or on paper. To review, read p. 187 in *New Directions in English 5*. Make a list of all the pronouns listed on this page, on pp. 47-48, and on p. 219. Now you should be able to recognize all the pronouns.

Read the paragraph below and substitute pronouns for any noun or noun phrase which seems repetitive or unnecessary:

> Mr. Jones built a swimming pool on the roof of Mr. Jones' apartment building. The swimming pool was beautiful, and Mr. Jones was very proud of the swimming pool until the swimming pool began to leak. Soon, water was dripping down from the ceiling to the floor on every story of the building. From top to bottom, the apartment building was thirteen stories tall! All the people in the apartment were angry and all the people in the apartment complained to Mr. Jones. Mr. Jones drained

03-1 (5A)

65

3 (continued)

the pool and made the pool into a basketball court. The people in the apartment building were happier, and Mr. Jones was happier too.

Read your new paragraph to a partner. Are there any places where you can't decide which noun was replaced by the pronoun? (A good rule is that the noun should be mentioned once before you substitute it.)

---

4   Do the Activity Sheet. Hand in your completed work to your teacher.

OBJECTIVE

Identify and use pronouns correctly.

1503-1 (5B)

PLAN *Copyright © 1969, 1973 by Westinghouse Learning Corporation. All rights reserved. Authorized for use only with PLAN* Educational System. Printed in U.S.

Words That Substitute

ACTIVITY SHEET

Part 1

Draw a line under each pronoun.

Johnny got his beautiful new bike for a Christmas present. He loved its shiny-red paint and beautiful black tires. He polished and cleaned his bike everyday at first, but soon he got lazy. Too often, he let its tires go flat and its frame get dirty while he played street games with his friends. They often borrowed his bike and dented its fenders. Two years later, Johnny found a picture of himself and his new bike, compared it to the wreck on the front porch, and felt very sorry.

Count the pronouns you've underlined.

How many refer to Johnny? _____

How many refer to the bike? _____

How many refer to the tires? _____

How many refer to Johnny's friends? _____

How many refer to the picture? _____

Part 2

Write the correct pronouns above the **boldfaced** nouns or noun phrases.

Johnny wondered whether **Johnny** could fix **Johnny's** bike up again.

Johnny saved **Johnny's** money and put **the money** into a bank. Then

Johnny bought some paint and painted **Johnny's** bike after knocking out

all the dents in **the bike's** fenders. Then **Johnny** compared the picture to

Johnny's bike and was satisfied again.

OBJECTIVE: DEMONSTRATE VOICING TECHNIQUES IN A SPEECH BY VARYING THE
PITCH, RATE, VOLUME, AND FORCEFULNESS OF YOUR VOICE. YOU
SHOULD EXERCISE PROPER ARTICULATION, PRONUNCIATION, AND
PROJECTION.

LEARNING ACTIVITIES	OPTIONAL RESOURCES
KEY WORDS: *pitch, rate, volume, forcefulness, articulation, pronunciation, projection*	

(a) Included in this Objective are
the basic oral skills necessary for an
effective presentation. In a speech
text, study the section that explains
the use of voicing techniques. Do you
understand the difference between pitch
and rate, volume and forcefulness?
Listen to a recorded speech for these
skills.

(b) The most effective way of analyzing
your own use of these techniques is to
listen to your voice as recorded on
a tape recorder. You might like to
experiment by recording a conversation
between you and a friend and then
comparing it with a recording of you
reading the conversation of two
other people. You could find such a
conversation in a short story or play.
Do you use the same intonation in
both cases? If so, which delivery
would you consider more effective and
why? If you don't have a tape
recorder, the same experiment can be
performed by having a friend listen
to the spontaneous conversation
and the "conversation" read from a
script.

For maximum effect, have the evaluator
look away while you speak so that
his judgment will depend solely on what
he hears.

(a) Speech In Action, Record Album
(Scott, Foresman)

(a,c) Speech In Action, K. Robinson
and C. Lee (Scott, Foresman 1965)
pp. 108-135

(a,c) Modern Speech, J. Irwin and
M. Rosenberger (Holt, Rinehart &
Winston 1961) pp. 52-93

(a,c) Speech For Today, Hibbs et
al. (McGraw-Hill 1965) pp. 201-223

(d) Great American Speeches,
Volumes 1-4, LPs or Cassettes
(D. C. Heath, Indianapolis, Indiana)

-1-

101

LEARNING ACTIVITIES	OPTIONAL RESOURCES

The evaluation form attached to
this OLU will help focus your listener's
attention on whether or not you, as a
speaker, have mastered the aspects of
speech which are emphasized in this
OLU. Ask a classmate who is also
preparing a speech to make the
evaluation.

(c) Read the section in your speech
text describing proper articulation
and pronunciation. Can you think of
any errors you make in articulating
or pronouncing words? Remember
that when speaking before a group,
extra care should be taken to pronounce
each word correctly and to avoid
running words and sentences together.
Practice pronouncing each syllable
distinctly by reading an article
aloud. If you have a tape recorder
available, you might tape your
reading and analyze your results by
listening to the playback.

(d) The most effective way to insure
the maximum use of voicing techniques
is to orally rehearse your speech
several times before actually presenting
it. Thus, you can concentrate on
placing the emphasis where it is most
effective and identifying any words
or sentences that present pronunciation
or articulation problems. A tape
recorder would be most useful at this
time; however, you may have a friend
or parent listen and offer suggestions
that would help eliminate any weak
points in your presentation.

-2-

102

Name of Speaker _____

Please rate the speaker, according to the following scale, on the items listed below.

Scale of 1-4:

1. Poor

2. Fair, needs improvement

3. Good

4. Excellent

Items to be evaluated:

Projection

Articulation

Pronunciation

Pitch (Does the student vary the pitch of his or her voice?)

Rate (Does the student vary the rate of his or her delivery?)

Volume (Does the student vary the volume of his or her voice?)

Moire Fun

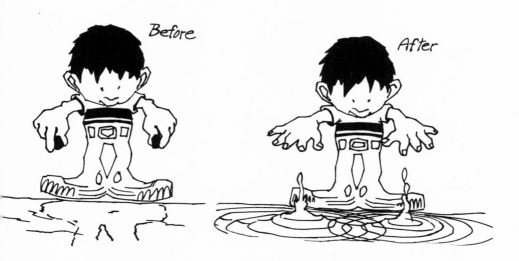

OBJECTIVE

Describe visual interference patterns. Explore the Moiré pattern cards.

---

1 Examine each individual card in the box of Moiré patterns. How many cards of each pattern are there? Match the pairs of cards (one white and one clear) with the same patterns on them.

---

2 On a separate sheet of paper, write down the pairs of numbers 11-11, 12-12, 13-13, 14-14, 15-15, 16-16, 17-17, 18-18 in the left margin. Leave three or four lines between pairs of numbers. Now examine each pair of like-numbered Moiré cards put together. See if you can center one exactly over the other. Then move them around and turn them so that the patterns seem to grow and move. See if you can describe each pattern in words on your sheet of paper. If you can, draw lines showing the general character of the patterns.

---

3 Have your teacher show you a piece of Moiré silk. What pair of Moiré cards look like it? Examine each card in that pair; pick up the clear one and look at the white one through it to see how the pattern comes about.

4   Fill a pan halfway with water at the sink or work table. Now drop two pebbles at the same time near the center of the pan. Look at the moving pattern that is made. This is called an interference pattern. The circles of waves from one pebble interfere with the circles of waves from the other and make this pattern. Drop pairs of pebbles farther apart, then closer and closer together, and watch what happens.

What pair of cards do you think will make this interference pattern? Try different pairs until you find the right pair. (Repeat the pebble experiment if necessary to refresh your memory.)

5   Look up **Light Interference** in an encyclopedia. Find some pictures of light interference. (Ask your teacher for help if you need it.) Is there a pair of Moiré cards that looks like one of the pictures? Perhaps a small section of a pattern looks like part of a picture. Does light from two sources act similarly to two pebbles dropped in the water?

6   See if you can find posters that are made using Moiré patterns. Can you think of anything else you've seen that may have looked like these patterns? Watch window screens as you walk down the street. Keep your eyes open for examples and make a list of at least five you have seen. Give the list to your teacher.

OBJECTIVE

Describe visual interference patterns. Explore the Moiré pattern cards.

2839-1 (5B)

OBJECTIVE: DEFINE AND USE THE FOLLOWING TERMS AND NOTATIONS: *relation, function, mapping, image, f(x), f:x → f(x), domain* and *range.*

Examples: A. 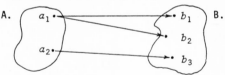 B.

1. Given the above mapping of a relation:

   a. Does the mapping describe a function?
   b. What is the domain?
   c. What is $f(a_2)$?

2. Given $f:x \rightarrow 2x + 3$, $x \in R$, does f describe a function?

3. Given a function h defined $h(4) = 2$, $h(9) = 3$ and $h(16) = 4$, what is the domain?

LEARNING ACTIVITIES	OPTIONAL RESOURCES
KEY WORDS: *mapping, function, relation, domain, range, image, notation: f(x), f:x → f(x)*	

(a) Definition of Terms. Carefully read each term and definition so that you may correctly pair elements in each set.

1. domain

2. range

3. $f:x \rightarrow f(x)$

4. image

5. mapping

6. function

7. $f(x)$

8. relation

a. Any set of ordered pairs of numbers
b. Set of all first coordinates
c. Set of all second coordinates
d. A relation which assigns to each element in the domain a single element in the range
e. A symbol to designate the unique element in the range of "f" associated with the number x in the domain
f. The set of all points which occur as values of the function $f(x)$
g. Pairing of elements of one set with another
h. A symbolism used to show the element of the range that is paired with a particular element of the domain

Check your work with a classmate.

- 1 -

LEARNING ACTIVITIES	OPTIONAL RESOURCES
(b) Using terms and definitions you have learned above, complete the following.	Algebra-Its Elements And Structure, Book II, J. Houston Banks et al. (McGraw-Hill) pp. 221-229

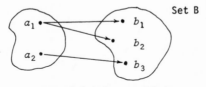

Set A   Set B

	Modern Algebra And Trigonometry, Mary P. Dolciani et al. (Houghton-Mifflin) pp. 208-249:1971 Ed., pp. 340, H-K:1965 Ed.

1. Elements of Set A are called _____.
2. Elements of Set B are called _____.
3. Demonstrate a mapping from A to B.
4. Give an example of the notation: $f : x \longrightarrow f(x)$.
5. Name the image elements above.
6. Name all possible relations from the drawing.
7. Name several $f(x)$.
8. Is there a relation above that does not define a function?

Algebra-Book Two, A. M. Welchons et al. (Ginn) pp. 126-157

Elementary Functions, School Mathematics Study Group (Yale Univ Press) pp. 1-38

A Function Is A Mapping, Film, 11 min. (Modern Learning Aids)

(c) 1. Define the domain and range for $\{(x, y) : y = 2\}$.
   2. If $P(x) = x^2 - 2x + 1)$, then $P(a^2) =$ _____.
   3. Define the domain and range for $\{(x, y) : |x| - 1\}$.

Introduction To Functions, Filmstrip (Popular Science Publishing Co.)

Relations And Functions, Filmstrip, 45 frames (Stanley Bowmar Co.)

(d) Optional: Prepare a 2' x 4' poster for the function $\{(x, y) : |x| - 1\}$. Compose a table of sample values for domain and range values together with a graph of the function.

Check your answers.

OBJECTIVE

Identify ways people show prejudice against other people.

Activity Sheet

Do the Activity Sheet. You may want to use a dictionary. Have a partner check your work.

2

The Rabbit Brothers

a. Look at the filmstrip.

b. Make a list of the things Joe Rabbit was prejudiced against. Are you prejudiced in these ways?

3

We Live in Communities, pages 140 through 141

a. Read pages 140 through 141.

b. Discuss how some people dislike or are afraid of people who are different from themselves.

4T

Man and His Cities, pages 57 through 60

a. Read pages 57 through 60.

b. With your teacher and a group of students, act out how people could show prejudice against the people you read about.

5T

The Difference Is the Same

a. Listen to the tape.

b. With your teacher and a group of students, discuss how the animal story says something about people. Do people always solve problems the way the little animals did?

6T

Write a paragraph in which you tell why the three animals in the story you listened to in Step 5 were not prejudiced against each other, even though they were different from each other. Show your paragraph to your teacher.

4318-1 (5B)

ACTIVITY SHEET

What does the prefix "pre" mean? For example, what does "pre" mean in the word **pre**fix? Use a dictionary if you need help.

What is this man?

What does the verb "to judge" mean?

What would "prejudge" mean?

What do you think it means to be "prejudiced" against something?

To be prejudiced against something means being down on something you are not up on! In other words, it means having a bad opinion about something without having a good reason for your opinion. For example, people who are prejudiced often dislike those who are different in some way.

4318-1 (6A)

HAROLD F. RAHMLOW is Vice President, Learning Systems, The American College, Bryn Mawr, Pa. In this capacity he is responsible for a program of learning research and development affecting 60,000 professionals in life insurance and related financial services. He earned his Ph.D. in education from Washington State University, where he subsequently served on the faculty. Prior to joining The American College, Dr. Rahmlow was a principal research scientist with the American Institutes for Research. He has served as Vice President of the National Society for Performance and Instruction (NSPI) and has authored many articles, presentations, and workshops.